Contents

PREFACE

The Day That Changed My Life

I can remember the feeling like it was yesterday. I felt trapped and frustrated, like a toddler stomping their feet and protesting against what they don't want in that moment; no amount of logic could get me out of the silent tantrum in my head.

Adults are very similar to children funnily enough. We just get better at disguising the same mixed rush of emotions under the surface and pretend to carry on with a smile.

It was during maternity leave with my second child that I felt trapped in the "normal" way of life that involved living to work to pay bills. My soul signed up for approximately another 25-30 years of "living the majority of the week waiting for the weekend" and battling through the weekdays to get the "job done" and keep food on the table.

I'm an experienced Engineer by profession so logic and theory are my comfort zone. The financial calculations based on our household incomes and outgoings was crystal clear in Excel-defined black and white in front of me, as they had been countless times before. Excel spreadsheets must tell the truth and can only report back what I tell them to do. Both my husband and I absolutely had to be work in order to keep the bills paid and food on the table. We had credit card debt of approximately £24k to be paid off, spread over roughly the next five years commitment. We had a mortgage, two car payments, child maintenance for our extended family each month and there was no way I could squeeze that out of my husband's income only. His wage wouldn't even cover the house bills and lights on. There was no alternative, and I could see no way out.

I stared at our household budgeting spreadsheet for hours and hours looking for a way to manipulate the calculations, feeling numb and helpless. I was confronted with previous life choices determining how to live my days, and my freedom to pursue my true desires taken away from me. The intense painful frustration came from that I couldn't see a way in the distant future to even change it slightly.

It would take a miracle.

Then a question entered my mind. "Surely there had to be another better way of living?"

And with the silence came the clarity and small voice inside knowing anything is possible.

I did not know how I would make it happen, but I believed it must be possible if I could just seek the right answers to my question and follow them with the right intended actions. In those moments of desperation, the hope and desire for a better way can deliver the start of a process and new way of thinking, where we never know where we will end up.

I knew the solution was based solely on fixing my mind on the end goal and manipulating the black and white numbers to unlock the solution. I just needed to start to use my imagination and throw away my current assumptions about how life had to be if I wanted a different outcome.

Slowly and surely my obsession with my goal lead my mind to be drawn to great books and speakers with one thing in common; knowing that their mind was their most powerful asset to shape their future. Everything begins in the mind with a single thought, good or bad, and then manifests in our world as a result.

We truly are the creators of our own reality, and when I woke up and remembered it that day - the journey for the Master Money Blueprint began that changed my life forever.

HOW TO USE THIS BOOK

Within all of us, at any moment in time, whatever point of our journey with money we are at, are the limitless resources you need to live a wondrous, happy and fulfilled life. One filled with time freedom and financial wealth.

Your problem is not that you are flawed or not good enough to have received the knowledge yet; rather you have not learnt yet the principles to return the power back into your life.

The sole purpose of this book is to teach you the powerful money mindset daily habits and mindful practices that will remind you of the power you have always had, and allow your days to be under your full creation.

The vast majority of frustration and pain in modern society is caused by the false reality that what we see is all there is. That simply is not the case, and a lie. A lie so strong that we know it deep within our soul, and that is why the pain believing it is so intense and against what we hope to gain from our life experience.

The truth is that we have all the freedom we need or want available to us at any moment. We just need to ask and believe it is coming. Freedom with money, time, energy, joy and abundance is all available when we simply open our eyes and minds to what is really there. It is opening all our senses to what is around us and seeing the abundance that is there already in our lives and always will be.

Money is just like any other living and breathing relationship in our lives. It is a resource in the bigger picture of life, but not the key component. We must learn to master and direct it, or it will control us. With the mastery of money as an example, our days ahead can be shaped with the activities and passions that matter most to you.

I believe that once you set the goal to have complete financial freedom, or any sort of freedom at all in your life, the world then becomes your playground to help others and create a lasting legacy with our only true precious resource - time.

We must understand that if today we are frustrated or upset with the way our life feels and looks right now, then our past daily habits and thoughts are not working and cannot get us to where we want to be. We need to act fast in new ways with the intention and dedication to change it immediately if we wish a different result in the future.

This book is broken down in to a natural path of beginning at any crossroads in any relationship, and then creating a new outcome ahead. These same principles can be applied to money, your health, your energy, your giving, even your personal relationships with loved ones.

In this book's context though, by taking full responsibility for our actions and thoughts that lead us down this original path, we move forward by addressing our past money thoughts and habits, redesigning our current beliefs and stories which shape how you feel today, and beautifully moulding our passion filled plans and emotions about your future. It is critical to look at money this way, like considering a committed relationship with a loved one, so that we can move forward with a change of attitude, mindset and purpose. How we feel and how we treat it will determine how it treats us back, determining the final destination and outcome.

Within each part of this book, there will be a list of actions that will change your mindset and feelings around money if you commit to them daily. I cannot make you do or try anything you do not wish to do, and it is completely up to you if you wish to follow them fully or in part. But know this as guidance - the results you experience are based completely on your application and commitment to the offered potential outcome of abundance and security of money in your life moving forward.

The daily habits and wanderings work completely, and will lead you to a life with financial freedom, if you follow them with your heart and mind fully.

The following principles within the book will take you to a new starting point for the rest of your life, with increased clarity around your purpose and how to make it a reality.

Keep these below points in mind as you begin:

1.   Commit to reading each of the 25 Principles in order at least once fully. They deliver the freedom and mastery of money described and are included for that sole purpose. They may seem small and insignificant, but the slight edge, taken consistently, is all you need to achieve far more than you currently dream of.

Think of a how a small flake of snow might eventually roll with momentum and direction into an avalanche.

2.   Ponder what is discussed and use inspiration to select the Principles in each season of your life (Past, Present and Future). Explore which you feel will bring immediate benefit to your mindset and life right now.

3.   Take part fully in the actions you feel inspired to try, and commit to practicing them for at least 7 days to see what change they bring to our life.

4.   Write down, each day, your thoughts and feelings as you read through this book. I strongly recommend you use a dedicated journal each day as you read and apply the principles, to fill with your inspiration and notes gathered upon reflection. This journal or notebook can also be used to start and end your day as part of a daily routine for optimising your life moving forward.

You will find this invaluable later on in your journey, and wished you had noted your thoughts at the start to reflect and notice the changes along the way. This journal will prove even more remarkable when you return back to it and see your goals have been achieved through your actions and commitment.

5.   Enjoy and re-read this book time and again when you feel you need it. Select new principles to try as your journey with money changes and deepens to one where you are in complete control. Very soon the techniques will become second nature, and then you will see that simplicity really is the key to habits that are life-changing.

A BOOK LIKE NO OTHER BEFORE IT

This book is unlike any other financial knowledge book you might pick up. There are countless books regarding the latest terminology and regulations around the physical management of your money, allowing you to learn basic concepts and terms that allow money to be moved from one location to another successfully.

This book is of a higher thinking and designed to create, through daily thoughts and actions, the necessary money mindset that will change your life and draw money to you for the purposes you wish.

Learning the mindset to succeed and focus on what you truly want will allow you to achieve anything in your life; not just financial or time abundance. Be prepared for this to kick start something even more fantastic when you know the power you have over something as small as money first of all.

CHALLENGE YOURSELF TO TRANSFORM

These principles that you will learn in a short space of time will change your life forever, but only if you apply them. You have the power to change your actions and destination of your life in any moment. All we have is the present moment, and remember this will be your greatest challenger.

Applying the principles ahead will most likely involve far greater effort than you have ever placed on a goal in your life. It may be uncomfortable, mentally or physically or both to change, but if you push through the rewards promised will appear.

You may even face life changing events that put everything you have learnt and practiced to that point to the test. I testify that if you stay true to the course you have begun, you will see a new mindset emerge that slowly will involve your whole life. Not just your money, but the changes that start to adjust the way you view the world and everyone within it for the better.

You will begin to realise that we are all on similar journeys, looking for meaning and purpose, but have been mislead to what the truth actually is, and creating false stories to keep us from failure.

This book will help you turn your potential power into a definite plan to hold the Master Money Blueprint that will create an abundance of financial and time wealth if you allow it.

Everything you read and ponder from this book is based on age old fundamentals of goals, planning and action as efficiently as possible.

There are no "Get Rich Quick" schemes included ahead, which only to give you results and then quickly die away. This is a lifestyle and mindset journey that will change your life forever if you allow it to.

This is the start of it.

THE MASTER MONEY BLUEPRINT

The Master Money Blueprint Principles are very simple and profound, built to transform your life as you begin your new journey to mastering money once and for all. If you follow them all fully, you will see rapid changes in your life overall and not just in terms of financial abundance, but in all areas of your life too.

Follow them initially for 7 days to measure the impact they begin to have. If you feel something is not working for you, return to it at a later date as you feel inspired.

Our journey will be chronological in direction much like life itself.

This journey is your own, and based purely on what feels right to you to action and test.

We will:

1.   **Forgive the PAST and remember it no more**

2.   **Be PRESENT always**

3.   **Create a freedom fuelled FUTURE**

INTRODUCTION

WHY IS THE MASTER MONEY BLUEPRINT NEEDED NOW?

The world is full of many books on the subject of personal development and specifically on the topic of money. How to obtain money, how to keep it and how to use it more efficiently accordingly to someone's own experiences and interpretation on their own reality. They describe ways to make it work for you, how to create multiple sources of income, how to use it to start global empire businesses and much more.

Why then would another book about money need to be written if everything has already been said needed to be successful?

Like in our own lives, our thoughts and actions have lead us directly to the moment we have arrived at today. If the strategies and mindsets already presented to the world still leave most people feeling powerless to money; fearful of it and the control it has over their lives; or even how it seems to shape fellow humans for good and bad, then something far greater was required. A deeper connection to see what money truly is had to be presented. A blueprint of how to use money as a slave to our commands, rather than our master. We would finally have the Master Money Blueprint to use that would open up our lives to the abundance of this source of energy that has, and always will, be within our grasp.

Contained within the few chapters are the key principles of this master mindset and suggested daily actions and beliefs that will change how you view your own power to create your present days and your future. You will unlock the eternal mindset that will deliver endless resources to you in terms of money, but also allow you to apply these principles to all areas of your life.

Money is simply the one focus area where the principles have been adapted and shaped, with specific actions that will allow you to feel joy and become the master of your money once more and for the rest of your life. The only way to see above what we currently believe is to have daily practices that raise our own internal thoughts to a higher level, in tune with the bigger picture of our lives, and become aware of where the source of all our external life possessions come from.

The exact eternal principles show the source of all life's energy is already within us, and you may find yourself frustrated that nothing new is written on the next chapters ahead. The reason why we struggle and suffer pain is when we chronically believe that the source of all our life's circumstances comes from external to us. The pain comes as we know fundamentally this is not the true, and everything we need to thrive and create a life of freedom is already within us.

This book's sole purpose is to help you reconnect with that inner knowledge of the source of all power and energy in your life once more.

WHAT STOPS US FROM THRIVING WITH OUR MONEY?

Our attention and time is our only true asset, yet we live in a modern world where we are constantly dumb to our surroundings and the present with constant distracts and notifications. The sole purpose of our life is to pursue happiness, and carefully select the elements that bring us the most joy whilst removing anything that brings us pain or suffering. This is the focus for our own life, but also living the higher calling of actively trying to help others achieve their goal as well.

When we are joyful, we are able to become our true self with the freedom that we crave.

Joy and happiness can be found at any moment within ourselves. However, we have forgotten that precious knowledge through the many distractions of the world and as a result, give the power of our own internal happiness over to material possessions such as money, success, our appearance, or other people. The truth is that we cannot have enough of what we do not need. When we believe that we need to have material, external possessions in order to make us feel worthy or happy, that is when any goal achieved and reached is always tainted with the sadness that the prize was not the goal indeed.

The acquisition of money or possessions need to be based around goals to truly provide joy and satisfaction. Money to enable a certain working life balance, or possessions which add real value will always trump money for the sake of a larger bank balance. Money requires a purpose to provide value.

Money is just another relationship within our lives. Once which we need to provide attention and cherish for it to thrive. As with any bad relationship, if we allow money to control us, it will do so with negative outcomes, and thus, we need to ensure we give it direction and purpose at all times, with the best intentions set for our well-being.

NATURE IS OUR GREATEST TEACHER

Through any struggles and stresses of life that are portrayed around us, remember to simply look to nature in its humble background to our lives as a gentle reminder of what is truly there. Nature does not know when a financial crisis hits our business global empires. Nature does not know that the prices of food processed for us to be convenient have been increased dramatically. Nature only knows and believes in the seasons of change, and the cycle and pre-planned destiny that it has within it to prepare and plan ahead, whilst also giving full energy to its present stage in its development.

The apples know only to grow from their seed once the tree is ready to support them, drawing nutrients from the ground and from the elements around it. They will continue to thrive and grow despite any financial crash that we might have forced into our limited sight. The roots will still continue to grow deeper to last through the autumn and winter, with the knowledge that Spring and Summer will bring another opportunity to bear good fruit for us to enjoy.

Like nature itself, the Master Money Blueprint draws from that eternal higher knowledge of where the true source of all our external manifestations in our life come from, and allow you to remain in that knowledge enlightened.

PART 1:

OUR PAST

Forgive the PAST
and remember it no more

In order for any relationship to be successful in the present and future, we must take full responsibility for our past errors in judgment and do them no more. We must forgive and forget any past mistakes made through lack of knowledge and choices; especially with ourselves, and realise that we are the only ones we have the true power to change the course of our future with a change of heart, mind and actions.

Money is one of the most highly emotional subjects we can face in our lives, and bring a whole range of mixed feelings from pure joy to immense pain and stress. Happiness and joy come usually from positive intentional actions, and those actions show our current priorities. How we use our money and resources shows what we value most and believe will bring us joy and happiness. If we believe the truth that our income represents who we are of value as a person, then the constant goal of chasing for more and more money or purchasing even greater more lavish external materials will never lead to fulfilment and happiness. There is always someone earning more than us, or someone worth more for doing less, and the endless loop of never quite reaching enough to ensure the constant level of happiness we desire will continue.

The value of your soul is worth far more than any income or price tag, but we must make sure that how we use our money represents what we believe brings true value to our lives today and moving forward.

Principle 1: Take responsibility for your starting point

Starting from today, choose to believe that the energy and focus we give to our money will be returned back to us. We have the choice to make that focus positive and work in our favour from now on. A lack of positive mindset or direction results in stopping any positive changes to our money mindset occurring, or even worse, our situation going becoming more negative.

The understanding of the energy of money and our relationship with it is similar to the Law of Electricity which we see physically when we create an electrical circuit to turn on a light or give us power. We cannot see electricity itself. We have no proof it is really there, yet we believe whole heartedly that when we attach an appliance to the electrical point that it will work. A number of factors are at play here to make that all happen. First, we need the circuit components within the device and electricity source to be functioning correctly, and then source power to be able to reach out home from a supplier. Quickly, we see our faith in electricity to always be ready for a device and never ending in its resources allows us to have the faith that the Energy can continue to produce more results if we have the source connected the right way. And indeed, further just like an electrical circuit, if we turn the connections of the positive and negative power source around, it will simply not work and energy will not flow. It is not that the power has not been delivered successfully to our home, or that the components inside the device are not working correctly - it is simply that we do not have the connection in the right order to physically allow the electricity to flow as it wants to. The source still remains there able to power the device, just we have physically prevented it from happening until we turn the electrical components the right way around.

Considering our money habits and relationship today, regardless of where your starting point is compared to others, we need to consider our full spending of our entire income. If your outgoings are more than your incoming, then your shortfall will be your downfall in life and lead to a road, slowly but surely, with financial pain and heartache. This simple truth is why so many people are in despair and fear that their money or lack of management of their financial increase is leading them deeper into pain, when they know that they should have made the choices to turn the relationship around long before the final warning signs appeared physically. They treated money as if it was their ruler, swayed by every desire to spend it or throw it away. They used money to make them feel better when they really should have been looking inside themselves for that happiness all along. And now, with the power given to the external object of money, the shift of power has happily been taken away from them.

The key to turning the worst of financial situations around or simply aiming for a better standard of management with your money is, regardless of income, making the absolute most joyful decisions for today and our future with the resource. To cherish money that comes your way in whatever form that might be, but with a healthy respect for it. Know that we are now the master of the resource and choose how we use it to fulfil our life purpose and desires.

Thoughts become things and yet again we are reminded here that our past internal and external language around money has shaped our present day. Any words that you speak in direct relation to money or resources lead to how we feel about them. Outside of our minds and external factors, our words are our most powerful tool to reshaping and changing our future.

If we were in love passionately with someone, how would we talk about it? If we wanted the best for them, would we resent them with words? Would we call them names and say how much they are not fulfilling our needs and how much of a struggle it brings us? Of course not, but yet we do this with money and our external resources all the time. We label money as if it is scarce and running out, or that the items it can purchase provide joy and fulfilment. We either spend it too quickly, or hold onto it for dear life within multiple bank accounts and refuse to spend a penny even when our basic needs should be met. Frugality is an important attribute of a successful money relationship, but not with the language that means we feel it could run away from us if we let it out our sight.

Our money is merely in our possession and stewardship to show how we treat it, much like every other resource such as our time, body, mind, health and loved ones. If we steward over money and carry out the correct principles and actions with a small amount, then the world will reward us with more to manage correctly. Think of your household and life spending as an intended directional flow between money, yourself and the rest of your life ahead. Make every penny count and give it a purpose without leading to suffering for you, your family or others long term. Every penny should clearly show your financial goals and direction you wish for your life, with as much as possible automatically sent to the correct place to look after it well on your behalf.

Frugality and expensive taste have a place within every household, and your priority is to make sure your resources, including money, are balanced and show what you want to be. Spend less on the things that don't matter and balance with spending with style on the things that do matter and will last the test of time such as love and connection.

Looking at your current spending habits. Be proud of any positive strengths you have already shown to others and yourself, and make sure you focus on creating more of those in your life. If you have the good habit of helping others, then continue to do so and even aim to increase that slowly by surely whilst not bringing suffering to yourself or your family. If you have the good habit of investing in your future without fail, and you can see that money working for you whilst you sleep to generate more money, be proud of the fact that you are becoming the master over your finances and telling it where to go to do the work for you.

Display your incomes and outgoings as a sign of what you value most in life and your goals. Start any day afresh with the promise that you will reverse engineer from those goals, and seek out ways to make sure you are committed and achieve them.

If your outgoings include any forms of borrowed money from others, whether this covers your basic needs of shelter and safety or otherwise, take full responsibility from this day forward to know exactly how much you are indebted to that provider and how you can make it right with them as quickly as possible. Even if it is painful and uncomfortable, without this full responsibility, we cannot shift our past if we do not face the reality of where we stand in debt to others. It is now the time to make those things right once more. We will discuss more on key habits that can do this, with remarkable commitment and passion, to erase those bad habits of not being self-sufficient from your life.

Principle 2: Commit to a life with abundance and responsibility moving forward

Whilst our focus remains in removing our past mistakes as shadows on our present-day living, we must commit to a life filled with thoughts and actions that confirm the abundance of freedom with external resources we know to be true.

Having faced our responsibilities and know our current situation, we must now commit to making those same mistakes no more and setting a new higher standard for living and our relationship with money.

This is a simple principle to put into place, but often comes as a result of a hard lesson with either intense pain or suffering. Realise though that if you are in debt to another at this time, you are not able to live freely as you are intended to. Even though the pain and suffering might be manageable with our current circumstances, we have to look forward to being free from it with commitment and passion.

Principle 3: Eighteen Days of Living Expenses created for the new habit of planning ahead

If you have become indebted to others, requiring regular payments of your money and thoughts, the first action we must take is to set a new habit for never entering such agreements again. The only exception for this should be when we are seeking a safe comfortable shelter for ourselves and family, to meet our basic needs for protection in our lives. For any services we receive from others where we have the option to make regular payments or one total payment, the ideal should always be to plan for, save accordingly throughout the year and pay off in full in one amount with a thankful heart.

Make your first focus to create a small buffer fund of roughly eighteen days' worth of living expenses available to you immediately. This will allow you to cover any sudden emergency expenses that might arise in your life, without the past habit of borrowing from others. Eighteen days of living expenses, such as housing, food and water, would be the ideal as a first goal amount to allow for mental security, should you require to find an alternative source of income suddenly due to a change of circumstance in your life as well.

The aim would be that this money is used to prevent further debts being created whilst we fully right our past mistakes with money through borrowing from others money which was not ours and spending it.

Principle 4: Right your past wrongs

Having evidence of past wrong or bad decisions in any relationship will block any light of happiness and joy with one strong force.

There is absolutely no point in earning £1m a year if you spend £1.2m a year; you will go nowhere fast and be just as much a slave to the money as if you earned £10 a year and spent £15 instead.

Go to any divorce courtroom today and you will see no more common cause of families torn apart than when a couple are on different pages with their money relationships, and debt is one of those powerful destruction buttons. More often than not, debt is linked to money emotionally spent when we want to make ourselves feel better in the moment, and the good feeling lasts just as long as it takes the money to leave our wallet.

We want to feel worthy and loved. We believe the lie that what we have physically around will allow us to see our worth. The truth is that the real worth is inside us, but we simply forgot to look for it in the most obvious place.

Just like if we were to wrong another human with a misplaced word or action, causing them pain or upset, we must right all our past wrongs and make amends for them fully. Money habits of debt and spending more than we earn hold control and power over us, whether we like it or not. Owing others in any form as a debt to pay means we cannot fully live in our current moment, free to make any choices with our resources as we see fit. If we are indebted to another with our money, all the money earnt by our skills and talent and current value cannot stay within our own home and life.

If we are indebted to another for an income, then we are at their mercy and decision power for how much our time and effort is worth and when we can be free to do what we want to do instead. If we answer only to ourselves with all our money and time, then we truly are free to move, wander and live life as we feel inspired and joyfully so.

It is the only way to be completely free in the present and in our future.

Principle 5: Settle all personal debts with committed passion and thankful heart

When you are indebted to others or even setting new standards for yourself, meeting the minimum required with either your money, your time, or your efforts will only ever lead to minimum results. You will not excel to the heights you are capable of, and so with our resources, we must always aim to exceed our commitments to others and ourselves. Perhaps this will push us out of the comfort zone of what we believe we are capable of, but only then will we get a glimpse of what we are really capable of.

Do not look on any taxes or debt repayments with anger or resentment, as the thoughts and actions will only be amplified further into other areas of your life. Instead view all debts to be paid by pondering what the payment brings into your life instead, and pay with a thankful heart as much as possible.

If it is shelter and warm, be thankful for the safety and location to raise a family meeting their needs fully.
If it is taxes, be thankful for the services you enjoy and freedom of choice that the government provide you in order to live the life of your wishes without fear of mistreatment or control.

If it is money borrowed, be thankful for the opportunity to better your life through the purchase, but aim to repay it as quickly as possible. If you struggle to gain a thankful heart mindset with any form of debt paid, consider for a moment the people and actions involved in providing the service or product you are enjoying as a result.

If it is paying a utility expense for your home, think of all the people involved in giving you that particular source of energy and the time and effort put in to make sure it works whenever you need it, whatever the situation. Before making any payment, and if you find your mindset to a negative one, consider all those involved with the service you are to pay for a short time and watch as your heart opens up with thanksgiving for all they have done for your comfort and safety.

Principle 6: The 10% Rule

Always go above and beyond the minimum requirements of yourself in terms of money for any debts owed to show thanks for the funds but also to remove the burden from your life as quickly as possible. The Law of the "10% Rule" will be your greatest tool here to actively and easily remove effort and hardship from acting on this very principle with style.

By adding on 10% extra to the minimum payment requested of you, you can remove time spent in debt, reduce dramatically the interest paid over and above the amount borrowed to your debtor, and achieve the happiness of knowing you are not only meeting your minimum requirements but overachieving them. Add on this ten percent extra to any monthly payments due that keep your home and family safe. This automatic action on any payments to others that are a standing agreement for service provided or loan received will see you make over one full extra payment a year to them if honoured each month, allowing you to show yourself as an honourable person who takes responsibility and thanksgiving for the services they receive from others. The same respect and honour will then return back to you in other ways in your world.

You may even seek to set a higher standard of meeting twenty percent extra on top of any payments to be made. This surely would be in your favour if you were not seeing any other areas of your life suffer as a result. This action alone will drive your success with your relationship with money and security within your life at least increasing 80% more, all shown by the Natural Law of the Vital Few.

Principle 7: The Double Down Snowball Method

If you face many debts within your past still acting as shadows on your current day and controlling your actions in some way, you may find the next method of debt payment to be the most beneficial to gaining joy whilst committing to the responsibility for your actions.

Begin with a piece of paper and with all your debts written down in descending order from largest to smallest. Make a commitment to make the minimum payments, ideally with ten percent extra included as your new standard, on each of them as a first step. Commit to adding the ten percent of the value on any debts where you can manage and life will not suffer. With your smallest debt, aim to give as much as you can to that debt only, and send that payment with a thankful heart. Continue to do this until the smallest debt is paid off in full. Then with that debt removed from your life completely, and a vow to never enter that debt again in any form move to your next smallest and repeat the process again until it is removed completely.

You will quickly find that your debts disappear faster than you had planned had you not committed to a joyful heart and actions when paying your debts, and quickly will have the reality of living completely on your terms and achieving total financial and time freedom.

PART 2:

OUR PRESENT

Be PRESENT Always

The only thing that is truly real in our lives is our interpretation of what we see in each moment. A fleeting moment that either we can choose to feel joy or pain by what we interpret around us. Our relationship with money in the present and how we treat it will shape the future ahead of us.

To understand fully our present, we must be actively working to remove as many shadows of our past today, so that our future will be free from them. Consequently, we can feel the freedom that is within us all at any moment by focusing on the elements of our life that truly make us feel happy and seeking more things which drive those same feelings. When we are present and happy, we realise the abundance and beauty of life that was already there in front of us, but were too distracted to see before.

In the next principles ahead, these will all bring us back to the present moment, highlighting what we have already around us and what is truly real.

The habits will align with what we know to be true deep within us regarding our lives and our greatest hopes for the future.

Principle 8: Understand the Energy of Money

On a fundamental level, everything we can physically see and touch is made of energy. Broken down on an atomic level, each smaller and smaller particle making up each cell or atom acting as building blocks of the universe vibrates at a certain frequency in order for you to tell it apart. Light for example, vibrates at different frequencies so that you can tell what colour it is and its purpose. You know it is a police car from the blue light flashing, but fundamentally it is a light pulsing at 610–670 THz that our brain coverts to mean "blue". The light used to take photographs of your internal bones and systems vibrates at another exclusive frequency of $3 \times 10\ 16 - 3 \times 10\ 17$ Hz, small enough to effectively "see through" your skin and surface. The use of light around us has truly changed our modern life and without the visionaries before us believing in the power of light, we would not have the health or lifestyle advances we enjoy today.

Our thoughts and actions similarly send unique vibrations into our world that we can see, with happier uplifting joyful thoughts operating at the highest level. That is why when we are happy the world seems to feel better, more good things keep coming our way and offer more exciting opportunities for us. When we focus on the opposite or feel the opposite though of negative thoughts that make us feel sad or upset, it seems like the world is filled with the exact same frequencies of opportunities too.

Think about the analogy of purchasing a new car. When we are driving around in our normal lives, our new or current car colour and exact make seems to keep appearing on the roads ahead of us. However, the moment we change to a different car the same thing happens again. This is because our brain will naturally draw or see the things we think about most and with our car as an example, this means we see ourselves using a particular colour and model and see it around us more clearly as a result.

Our relationship with money like every other object we can touch, see and feel in this world and has its own unique frequency and power to draw or repel similar to itself, and even more important, our associated thoughts behind it. If you believe that money is hard to come by through childhood with your parents always fighting over money being lacking, you then grow believing money then is negative and causes pain in families. The money you then have in your possession will also share that frequency and deliver those opportunities back to you. You will find money to be a struggle, or believe people who have a lot of money must be mean or horrible to others. If you grow up believing that money was restricted and when you asked for the latest toy, were told "we don't have enough money for that!" every time, you might feel like money is scarce and should be protected and spent quickly in order to prevent it going away for good. If, on the other hand, you grew up seeing your close family members sharing money freely, giving to others without looking for it to be returned back and seeing money as a positive influence to help others, the chances are that you also believe that money is a positive tool and freely available to help others and yourself.

Our subconscious thoughts are the key to what we create and see in our life, and those deeper thoughts are driven by the thoughts we believe to be true. When we allow the voice in our head, our thoughts, to keep telling us one way regarding money is correct - we will continue to believe it. If we choose to act and think in the opposite way, the opposite will occur. This is called the Law of Attraction or Law of Emergence. What we believe and plant seed of in our thoughts and hearts will emerge into the world around us sooner or later. As Einstein said, time is relative and even though there might be a time delay between a thought and the physical evidence - it always will appear unless we shift it back to the course we wish.

Just like seeing your current car on the road, everyone's beliefs will be different, but allow them to see the world in a certain way and not easily deviate from it without new overwhelming evidence for the opposite.

Principle 9: Create a safe, orderly, peaceful and loving home for you and your family.

Maslow's hierarchy of needs is a key mindset theory comprising of a five-tier model of human needs often shown as a simple five stage pyramid.

At a fundamental basic level all humans require their physical needs of shelter, food, water, heat, clothing, sleeping and reproduction to be present and met in a sufficient way so that they can survive. That is purely to survive of course, and in order to thrive further we need to add all elements possible into our lives to truly become who we are met to be.

This pyramid states:

Basic level 1: Physical needs of Shelter, Food, Water, Heat, Clothing, Sleep and Reproduction needs met.

Safety Needs Level 2: Source of income, Personal Safety, Health.

Love and Intimacy Level 3: Friendship, Family, Connection to others.

Esteem Level 4: Respect, Recognition, Strength, Freedom.

Self-Actualisation Level 5: Desire to become the most that one can be.

We will learn principles that will allow you to realise all the elements of your needs, but must start our present-day journey with the most important element. We must meet our physical needs of safety, shelter and physical resources sufficient for our true needs. Before we begin our journey to shaping our future life, our sole purpose needs to focus on creating that safe, calm, loving environment that is our daily shelter from the outside world. A calm, peaceful and orderly home that allows our mind and body to relax fully from any external pressures that it might have faced and become our holy sanctuary.

In monetary terms, our first priority for any day must be that our home is kept within our possession at all times, and we are able to provide our basic needs for heat, comfort and good nutritious food and water. This will enable our mind to be clear and active to see how the world really is, and allow us to feel the inspiration to do our lives' work each day. A place for meditation on what matters to us most, and then the ability to take action without distractions from modern day life as much as possible, is important. Our time and focus are our gift and that must be our upmost priority to maintain in our home.

Clutter and distraction, whether physical, mental, emotional or spiritual, will only prevent our thoughts being inspired and directed to the life that we want to feel each day. Clutter takes away our attention by engaging our senses with something other than our own thoughts and decisions. When we have little or no opportunity to be with our own thoughts and actively choose the thoughts we wish, our life starts to be reactive rather than proactive.

Maslow's Hierarchy mentioned above is profound for many reasons, but none more so that the realisation that in order to thrive once our basic needs are met, we need a method in order to keep those things in our life such as a job or money source; all the other levels in the thriving pyramid can be met purely by our actions alone without further input from our surroundings or resources. Quite easily, it can be seen after having those basic levels met sufficiently, you can progress further with your actions up the pyramid to reach the freedom you desire and become person you wish to be. It is only our distractions and altered incorrect beliefs that make us believe we need anything more than this in order to thrive and exceed our current situation.

Seek to own completely your own shelter as your upmost priority in the present to ensure you and your family are able to thrive without question. Search your soul to make sure your current location and home feel like the best place for you to move forward in your journey, or if they are holding you back. Eliminate as much clutter and distraction from your life as possible without affecting your basic needs being met to fully to open up your home once again to be the sanctuary it should.

Give away to others who can love them more any clutter or items in any form that no longer bring you joy, but instead distract your mind and dilute the good loving feelings that should always be present in your home.

Seek to make your home your shelter. Your peaceful, restful dwelling and comfort once more.

Principle 10: Become who you want to be, do the things you want to do, and feel how you want to feel today.

Like a painter starting a masterpiece, we begin the next series of Principles finally realising what our purpose for life will be by tapping into our true feelings and thoughts in our subconscious. This will not be as painful as it might sound, and through a simple process of distracting and meditating for just long enough to gain the information, this will allow us to gain the necessary financial and time freedom to live it in reality.

The Principles work by discovering your money and lifestyle visions for your future and the type of person you wish to become, with priority given to what actually would make your life feel good with no regrets. After you complete this process, your needed money and resources to make this happen will come together naturally in your life as inspiration or choices.

Regardless of your budget or your current financial state, you will find this first section critical to your life success when applied consistently and whenever you feel at a crossroads in your life. We will be focusing on a holistic view to our life, and you will see all resources are intertwined together rather than separate in the larger plan for your life. Like the painter beginning his work, we must be comfortable to know that we may only receive the background colours with our current understanding but slowly and surely the finer details of the painting will open up to us when we are attracted to the activities and thoughts that feel good.

Often, we spend too much time being passive by-standers in our own lives, swayed every moment by the next thing to grab our attention and notification on a device.

Our daily thoughts shape our future life.

What we think about becomes what we do.

What we do daily becomes our lifestyle.

Our lifestyle then becomes our legacy.

What do you genuinely want out of life?

Not the society answer for your life, or what your parents or peers thinks, or even what your children and partner might want. We should not let the fact we do not know the answers, or have not pondered this before in our life, but asking our self is key to living a fulfilled life designed on your terms.

Can you see yourself achieving your life time goals slowly but surely?

Without goals and standards to aim for, we are like a small boat being blown every which way the wind takes you. We quickly become lost or even frustrated with our course.

Look at your daily life as it stands right now. If you had endless resources of money and time, would you live each day exactly as you do right now? Would you work where you work, or eat what you eat, etc? All it takes a desire for a better structure that fulfils you to slowly but surely start to see it taking shape in your life.

Our only real asset of worth is our time. Are we using our most precious resource on the loves of our lives, or are we using it up on the things that actually do not matter to us long-term? Sometimes, the only clarity we have is the change we want to make, and the direction we want to head, without knowing how we make it happen.

As just like a strong magnet, the stronger those reasons why, the higher the likelihood of the ideal being achieved. You need to know the vision ahead for your life will be strong enough and bring joy to your soul in order to keep looking straight at it when the bumps and trials in life come.

Principle 11: 3 x 3 Pages

The technique of writing 3x3 pages allows you to get back onto the path of creativity and away from the fears and logic that might hold you back and stop their progress. To begin, find a quiet location where you can be free from distractions and have the time to focus. This process may take 30 minutes to complete, but sometimes longer. Perhaps go for a walk, spend time with your loved ones, or time with your loved animals to prepare your mind with what feels good already in your life before starting. Write as if the time has gone exactly as you want it to and as you aim to fill up three full A4 pages. Many new ideas will pop into your head that you haven't thought of previously. Be as specific as possible with as many details as you can regarding how you feel and what you see around you in the vision. Keep it positive, focussing on the ideal only and only list those things you want to happen.

By being conscious to describe in details our happiest life ahead in terms of 30 years, 10 years and 1 year, we will be able to then make that a reality through our actions.

Ponder for a moment and begin to form exactly what your ideal life would look, like paying particular attention to how you feel and the details of the surroundings around you in this imagined future.

Think about:
What time would you get up each morning?
Would you work for an employer or have your own business and set your own hours?
Would you perhaps even work full time or part time?
Would you do the school run or pickups, or would your partner do that half the time too?
What food would you eat for breakfast, lunch and dinner to feel great and healthy?

Would you exercise and what time would you ideally like to do that each day?
Are you in a particular room of your home or doing something that you love?
Describe in detail who is with you in the picture you see?

Starting with a blank piece of A4 paper, write the date 30 years from today's date exactly. This letter will be from yourself by 30 years older.

Start by writing your age in the style of "I am 67 years old and looking around me I see…."

Whilst in writing flow, try to include your WHY and HOW it will make you FEEL.

For example, you could write "I am currently 67 years old and looking round me, I see my dining room table with my family of two boys and their families. I am my ideal weight and feel strong and healthy. I can run around with my children and grand-children all day and do anything I want based on my desires rather than health or energy levels."

Next with a new piece of paper, do the same process, but this time date it for ten years' time from today, writing back to yourself today as if everything you hope will happen has already happened in similar close detail.

Start your second group of papers with the wording like this "I am currently (10 years' time from now your age) and looking around me I see…." Then let your words flow for three pages of writing. Describe how you feel, what you have around you, who you have around you, where you live. Make it as detailed as you feel you need to be to convey the scene that makes you feel good.

Finally, do the same dating a third lot of A4 paper with the date one year from today and continue for three full pages of writing.

Begin by writing "The date is currently (1 year from now) and looking around I see…" beginning the detail of your surroundings and feelings again. In a year's time you could see yourself with a new business starting, or a new child being born. Whatever you feel could be in your future that inspires you, write it all down for three pages.

This may take some time and the process may be completely alien to you right now, so be patience and enjoy it.

Keep these three letters stored in a journal or notebook for the time ahead, and perhaps even to treasure for the years ahead to look back on and see how much was accurately created.

This process has the power to change your life if you let it. The exact visions you have written now may not be how things turn out eventually. However, more often when our vision is very specific, life will open up for us exactly as we hope for. These visions however are fluid like us, free to change and adapt as they need to or even grow bigger beyond our initial visions. That is the beauty of time and our thoughts. Although our thoughts become our reality, when we feel them regularly with intense emotion of any sort, the time delay to turn the thoughts into our reality is there to make sure we are certain of the choices we are actively creating.

From the work of this particular principle, you will then start to see pictures in your mind of what life will look like. This would be an ideal time to remain in that focus and seek out photographs and visual images that you can keep with you at all times or display on a board within your home of what life will look like. This is called a Vision Board, and the combination of visual, written, thoughts and using all your senses as much as possible will allow the vision to take shape even faster in your life. Make the dreams come alive with all your efforts and might.

Principle 12: Your "Soul Words" Creation Session

Any vision that makes us excited or joyful about our future and what we can create consists of three key components. By looking for these three components and focusing on them fully committed, they will lead to your ultimate success and fruits of that success manifesting in your life.

We have touched upon these components before: how you would feel, who you would be, and what you would do if you were fully living the goal or vision you have for yourself. Every single person is unique, with different talents and passions, and every goal will be different for your own life and for someone else's. However, those core components will remain the same for everyone. These components are incredibly important as most people will focus on the doing (action) and less on how they feel, and rarely on who they are being.

When people have a vision - for example, to have a thriving business generating an endless resource for your life, fulfilled by helping people with that business and a loving large family around you to enjoy it – they would consider only the activities they need to do to achieve that. They need to find lots of customers, charge a good amount of money and then have a large home for their family to live in. However, when we come from a place that doesn't inspire and drive our feelings that we are missing, such as love and happiness, the destination ends up failing to bring exactly what we thought it would. It can leave the person cold and desperate for the next goal to chase or even worse, left numb and wonder what they are doing with their time and how can they get to a goal which actually satisfies.

With your three letters beside you, take a moment and write down two columns on a new page. If you have not completed or chosen the 3x3 pages Principle 11 as one to test so far, please aim to do this before continuing with this principle. You can complete the next described actions without it, but you will find it more beneficial and successful if you have chosen already to complete your 3x3 letters to yourself from various stages ahead in your life.

On a new piece of paper beginning on the far-left hand side, write the word "Aspect" and the middle of the page write "Feeling". With your thirty-year time vision in front of you, look to see any key aspects of it that jump out as critical to achieve. It could be that you want to feel healthy and strong to keep living as productively as possible to enjoy your life. Write down an aspect as you feel inspired to.

On the right-hand side beside it under the second column, consider the questions "How does it feel to be in my ideal life as if it is happening right now before me?", "What am I receiving from others?" and "What am I having to do or be?". If you were surrounded by your family that loves you, then imagine yourself being hugged and kissed for example. Do not let your logic take over and start to need to know the how or why this will happen. Just allow yourself to feel it and make notes.

Similarly, now in the same rows, write the column "Activation" on the right-hand side. Think about and brainstorm as many activities you could do that would activate that same feeling within your life right now. It could be that the feeling of love from others you could receive as a thank you for doing something kind for someone else. If you want to feel more confident in your future self, as you see yourself standing in front of others helping them, you could write down a sport you used to play that made you feel confident to be part of a team or place as an individual. This list of activity is a power tool to learn and one you will find you need time and time again. The activity that we believe will allow us to feel a certain way will start to encourage the life we want, if we take action to follow that inspiration to do them consistently.

What we really are uncovering here, through both these exercises, is clear direction for daily habits or activities that we know we will feel the way we are missing right now. Our next goal will be to focus on committing to 1-3 of those activities and developing those feelings further in order to bring into reality the life we want. Money will then quickly become the tool whereby we can open up these opportunities in our live if we wish, and shift our whole relationship with it back into our control.

So many people in the world are busy just merely surviving or making a living rushing to enjoy their only two freedom days at the weekend, and it is time not to be one of them any longer. If we don't take hold of what we truly want, and design it and work towards it – we may well look back and realise ten years have passed us by and no longer are our dearest relationships the way we wished they were, or our health the way we really want it to be.

Principle 13: Your Life's Mission statement

The beauty that comes from knowing and creating your own personal Mission statement based on Principle 12 and then how we use the essence of that one statement that really encompasses who we truly are rather than a goal list, and how that one statement can keep us hooked on our true course even when the times are rocky and need our attention a little more.

The past few sections have all been ultimately leading to this point where we focus on having the end or our ideal destination in mind.

A personal mission statement does just that, and I will take you step by step through how to ponder and create one for yourself. I would suggest you display it proudly somewhere where you can see it and read it each day and night, and even look to have them written in your personal journal and a copy within your wallet for reading at free moments in your day. Ponder it and feel the power of knowing you can create your most joyful self in the process as you choose your daily actions that align with these words.

Like everything of course, your first attempt at a Mission statement may only the first draft of it and a work in progress, so we do not need perfection here. We only need a first step in the journey to making one happen.

A personal mission statement fundamentally describes your core values that drive your life and ideally, how you would like the important aspects of your personality and life to be remembered. If you have chosen to implement Principle 12, you can use the words and feelings described as the basis for your statement structure.

Your mission statement then reflects your uniqueness and life you are leading right now. Think about the feelings generated by your life values and use any key words to describe it. It could be words like joyful, focused, creative, proactive, self-motivating, love and the list goes on.

We all have a home, our health, our relationships and our contribution to the world as key elements that shape how we feel about ourselves and our happiness levels. Take those areas and write down key words that feel good to you that you would want to be remembered by, and any key phrases that summarise how you feel too.

The single-mindedness of such a statement and the following goals and actions that come from it are life changing, and the picture starts to become very detailed indeed. These principles in your statement will feel like they fit together like a jigsaw puzzle, as you can't have a clean and orderly home unless you are proactive and look after your mind and health to have the energy to do it.

By centring our life on these timeless, fundamental principles that you have written down, completing your statement is when everything starts to become very clear and very exciting. In fact, that is when freedom and power truly are in your hands now.

Use all your senses as you start to see your mission and life take shape in your mind.

Principle 14: The Micro-Joy Method to prioritize and sort absolutely anything

Our sole purpose in life is to seek happiness and use inspiration to take action on those feelings to encourage more of them. This is the same principle if we are concentrating on our relationship with money, our relationship with our body and health, our relationship with others and so on.

Any relationship you wish to improve all starts with recognising where we currently stand, taking full responsibility for the actions that lead us to this moment and then resolving to move forward, focusing on elements that bring us joy, whilst bringing no further suffering to anyone else including ourselves in the long term. A momentary joy or smile is not worth it if we fail to bring long term happiness from it as there will be no ripple effect or energy from it carried into our future. It is not the best use of our time or energy to concentrate on short term or fleeting moments. We are able to create our future and must use our minds and actions to reflect that knowledge fully.

To get the most out of this Principle, completing Principles 10, 11 & 12 would been committed to and fill us with excitement and joy at our life possible ahead, even if we are unsure how they will be achieved. We do not need to have the full detailed plan ready at this time as that will become clearer to us as we move forward.

The Micro-Joy method will be your greatest tool when you need to select what your highest priority for your time, energy, money and resources. It should be and can be used in any area of your life, be it physical, mental or spiritual. You can use this very method to eliminate personal expenses that are not required in your life at this moment, to using this method when removing clutter from your home, to create a peaceful comfortable shelter and safe location to retreat to each day.

With the focus on the actions and feelings that you consider your life's mission and goals, you would select and order the actions from 1 onwards. Using the number 1 beside the action or feeling determines that it has the highest priority for your attention and focus moving forward, and we should not progress onto number 2 until we feel we have completed it sufficiently and wishing to progress. This may take one day to complete and gain the feeling or it may take a month.

If you are using this method with physical items, you can tell if the item is to stay in your life or not by how you feel when you touch, feel and look at the item. If it does not give you joy and feel happy, please give it to others who would love and cherish the item instead. If the item holds much material value, then the positive lesson would also to recognise that we wish to move forward using our resources only on items or parts of our life that brings true joy but give thanks for the item in our lives in the past and the joy it might have brought at one time.

Use the Micro-Joy method to provide 1-3 focus actions and feelings that you will create daily habits on for the next 12 weeks ahead. The chances are that you will need much less time that 12 weeks to achieve the feelings you desire, but we need to give them time and a state of deadline to activate our urgency. The urgency should be driven by the fact that our life will benefit greatly, but we may need to encourage ourselves initially to believe that it is achievable, even if they initially feel a little daunting. It is only when we are out of our comfort zone that we really learn who we are meant to be.

Each day for the next 12 weeks, remind yourself of these feelings and goals you wish to achieve within the short space of time. Carry them, written down in a journal or a card, within your wallet for you to see often, and plan your following day with these actions included as the first priority with space for the rest of life to occur around it. An ideal strategy would be to look to achieve your 1-3 feelings and actions as soon as you can within your day so that you allow the good feelings to shape and remain all day long, thus encouraging more wonderful and joyful moments in the remaining waking hours.

The intention of the Micro-Joy Method is clear - with any interaction with an external object, person or internal thought you come across during your day, you make an active choice whether it leads you in the direction you want to go in life or not. If it does support your ideal life, then we choose to keep it until it no longer adds value to us. If we feel that we could live without something, then that is a good indicator that we have outgrown its purpose and ready for new knowledge and inspiration to take us to the next growth period in our life.

Principle 15: Ask exactly for the resources you need with purpose and intention.

This principle again will work for any internal or external resource and not solely with money. The intention behind the principle remains everlasting in what it achieves in your life by drawing what you need and can use wisely with purpose to bring joy to yourself or others. Any resources we ask for in our lives with a purpose should seek to bring joy only, and not for any other purpose.

With any thoughts or inspiration you receive to bring joy to your life or others, and you feel you require resources such as money to make them appear quicker, you must write down exactly your needs and the amounts required that would allow that to happen. Give the money requested to enter your world a purpose and a positive one at that.

We can use this principle in a number of ways:

1) You can use this principle when setting specific monetary value goals when you know the life you wish to lead following completion of your 3x3 pages in Principle 11. This will allow the energy of money required to start to be drawn towards you to create it. Be conscious of the money coming your way as your mind starts to subconsciously look for ways to bring it to you to create more joy in your life. For everything you wish to see in your future years, source the exact current day value needed to make that happen from the total full amount it would require. Write that goal down in a personal journal or keep it with you in your wallet to view it daily as you start to focus on drawing the money to you. Aim and create big, and be aware that there is an endless supply of all resources available to you. Fear and doubt are your only obstacles in stopping it appearing or taking longer to arrive physically in your world.

Plan ahead for any desires in your immediate and long-term future, creating a physical location for the money to be saved within as it appears. The bigger the goal, the longer this might take to appear, but continue with faith, penny by penny.

2) You can also apply this principle when you are looking to take each day to meet your basic needs and confirm exactly what that needs to be. By being thankful for what you have right now, you write down what you would need in order to maintain the life you have and then, with a thankful heart, what would allow you to test out activities and thoughts that might bring you more joy. Source the exact present-day money value for the items you need and would like to try, and this will start the process for your subconscious to draw that money to you in various ways. It could be through gifts or donations; it could be through a business idea; it could be by offering service to others.

3) When you are considering your short term 12-week goals, you can also assign monetary values to the experiences and activities that would change your life for the better. This could be having all debts settled, your home secured fully with no payments required, a passive income method that would allow you to use your time as you see fit without having to work for someone else with your time and more. Always create quiet, peaceful moments without distraction after you have begun using this Principle, as your subconscious mind will place thoughts and reminders into your daily life that will require prompt action. It is then our responsibility to act on those promptings with due attention and effort once we have been given the knowledge we need in order to make the money appear in our life.

Principle 16: Carry physical money with you at all times

With more of the world encouraging us to be completely "cashless", allowing a piece of small rectangle shaped plastic such as a bank or credit access card to contain all the money you have in the world - we are losing access to one of the most powerful tools we have to change our money thoughts and vibration.

Physical cash has the strongest vibration and energy associated with it. You can touch it, you can smell it, you can see it and feel it between your hands and whenever you see it in your wallet you know you have money for your needs should you require it.

The act alone of going into your wallet and using your mind to spend the money contained in it, to buy a stranger a coffee or to buy a homeless person a meal, generates the same brain signals and joy feelings as if you actually had handed over the money and completed the action. That is the power of thought and physical items you see, and money is absolutely the very place where you can use this way of thinking to your advantage.

When we only contain cards, the first thought we believe when we open our wallet is that we are lacking in money as we cannot see it right away and that then results in our subconscious thoughts seeing evidence that money is missing in your life and hard to find. If you repeat this pattern of having no physical money within your wallet then you create more and more evidence outside of the wallet to support this.

You will find that each pay day money seems to come into your bank accounts but not stay long enough to last the month. You will find that whenever money appears in your wallet you will have the urge to spend it quickly or on purchases that do not bring you long term joy, as you believe it is scarce and hard to hold on to. If you still struggle to see the importance of this very principle, think back to a time of inspiration to help another person with money in some way.

You might have gone straight to your wallet or recalled in your mind your wallet empty with no physical cash. The inspiration to help out another human and make their life better could not be fulfilled due to the money habit you have developed, that you believed made your life easier to manage through small plastic cards instead. We missed out on the shared joy of helping another through a simple daily action without thinking of the future consequence.

Test out this principle in your own life and always aim to have physical notes and cash in your wallet every day when you use it. It can even be keeping the smallest paper note that the bank will give you in there at all times and still the mindset pattern will be created. Challenge yourself to see a future with even more physical money in your wallet and place the largest note you feel comfortable in your wallet to see it at all times when you open it, but perhaps do not spend it but instead in your mind spend it each time you go to the shops or see others in need.

The power of the mind is your most precious tool in changing your money mindset and this very action alone will prove to be very valuable to you.

Principle 17: Treat all money with respect and attention

When we show respect and love to any relationship in our lives, then it will return that favour and with interest. Money is no different to a physical human relationship between Parent and Child, even once our eyes are opened to the power we have over it. How you look after it, by keeping it safe and secure and respected, will see that returned back to us.

Consider currently how you store your physical money and other tools such as bank cards within your wallet. What does your wallet look like in shape, colour, material, appearance and smell right now? Hold it within your hands and really look at it fully at every angle and detail. Is it a cherished, loved item that was given to you, or purchased some time ago and loved and taken care of each time you use it? How are your physical money notes and change stored? Are the notes all lined up the right way facing you or are they thrown in and in a mess? Are your bank cards similarly looked after and present correctly inside or a pile stuffed into one slot? Do you keep all your forms of money such as credit notes and coupons in there to use and look after them?

The way we treat money is how it will treat us back.

Today is the best time to start to respect and look after your money with a deeper healthy love than before. Healthy respect being that we don't aim to protect it or hide it from everyone else, but are safe and secure to know that it is looked after well and will look after us well as a result. There is no jealousy or envy that can get into our mind as that would be the wrong type of love of money, and we aim for a higher appreciation that will change our lives positively.

One of the greatest tools with regards to our wallet and money handling is to take time to organise and sort it with respect and diligence. This initially might take some time to focus and sort, but then as you move forward to treating the wallet and items within it with your time and attention, the process will take a matter of seconds to maintain your new high standard. Arrange the physical items within it as you feel inspired, but looking at how you wish them to be respected in your life.

With the previous principle teaching us the importance of having physical money with us at all times to create more money into our lives, make sure that this habit is included in your wallet moving forward too.

Principle 18: Coloured envelopes of wealth

One of the most treasured Chinese traditions when handling money at celebrations involves certain colours and can change your feelings around money too.

The vibrant colours of Red and Green are key for their spiritual benefits both symbolising amongst other things mainly security, wealth, abundance and luck.

To use this colour in your own life in order to draw more of these attributes into your life, you may find placing small red or green envelopes into your wallet with small donations of physical cash in them so you can use them to give to others in need during your daily journeys. Knowing that it contains money as you open up your wallet combined with the eye-catching colour to prompt those feelings of abundance in your life subconsciously; you could then use the envelope to donate to others, thank someone for a good service given or buy a friend a drink and share time together.

That little small seemingly harmless envelope within your wallet, so subtle that no one might notice, will end up being one of the most powerful tools you keep close at hand when you are traveling in your daily life. The gift of giving to others even when we believe we cannot will be a great source of joy to you. The size of the gift, whether it be time or money in this case is not the objective, but rather carrying the envelopes will awaken your mind to looking for opportunities to give to others in a small way and show you have more than enough for your current needs so that you can complete the circle of giving and receiving.

If you feel right now that you cannot afford to place any money inside the envelopes, obtain one physical cash note and place it inside.

Then throughout your day in your mind as suggested before, see yourself handing it over to another person for their service in your life or as a thank you in appreciation.

Spend that money in your mind over and over again multiple times a day as you feel inspired, until the time comes where you feel you can give it away in reality.

Then refill another envelope and start the process again until you feel your needs are met and you can give to others.

This action alone, whether in mind or physically, will do more for your financial future that you realise.

Principle 19: The Drip Feed Method

We have already mentioned the 10% Rule within previously explained principles and the same can be applied moving forward when we have no debts but instead only services from others owed.

There is a wonderful phrase that goes along the lines of "how is it you cook a frog"?

You don't place the frog in boiling water, you place it in cold and slowly increase the temperature so it doesn't notice the difference.

In a roundabout way, we are creatures of habit and if you have chosen to apply some or all of the principles previously mentioned in your past and present-day relationship with money, we can use this principle to slowly but surely see what we are capable of and push ourselves to grow more than we might think we are capable of currently.

The Drip Feed Method is simply that little by little we are going to amplify our habits to new levels that will rapidly change your world to financial freedom.

If you committed to resolve all debts you have with others through money, applying the 10% Rule as a grounding first of all, you would then slowly every few months, or when you felt inspired to, increase that further by a small amount. The key is to make the increase small enough that your world can remain the same without any suffering to your basic needs.

Likewise, this principle should be applied with any money goals you set for yourself in the short term and long term. If you have a goal to create passive income for your life, that does not require you to work for another to generate money, you could likewise apply the Drip Feed method to the amount that you invest in that venture slowly but surely over time.

Reversing the principle, starting with the end goal in mind as a target, you can break down the steps into small one percent or similar manageable pieces to achieve the destination slowly but surely. Using this principle with others described such as visualising and displaying your goal as you work slowly to achieve each step will allow you to keep motivated when any trials appear that could have potentially held up your progress before. An example of creating the steps visually for you to see each day would be as simple as creating small boxes within your journal to colour or mark as you achieve them.

Using this principle, combined with the others discussed, will ensure your future will reach financial and time freedom much quicker than you would have previously thought as you have learned to master your money without emotional connection to it.

Principle 20: Prepare for new opportunities at short notice

Limiting our mindset to only what we can see will do more damage to our future that we can imagine.

Similarly, by not fully engaging the part of us that longs for our full self to be present in our lives at all times, through our daily actions and desires being met, does not allow us to contribute and co-create with others a more joyful future. Make a priority, once you are in a place where money is now under your control, to plan for new opportunities to occur at short notice in your life.

Create a location to place money sufficient for three to six months of income for you to have a safe, comfortable shelter to retire to each day and sufficient food and water for your needs. Look to keep the electricity flowing into your life only, and allow anything extra to be forsaken for a short time if temporarily required.

Knowing that you have this income saved aside for new opportunities or a sudden change in desires or course of your life will provide much security in knowing that your life is fully under your control rather than a victim of your circumstances.

Principle 21: Give of your time to the material and relationships that matter most to you.

A key principle that will change your resources, including money and also your attitude towards your present-day circumstances, will be to seek every day to give to others and grow from your current understanding daily. At the start of each day, ponder and begin with quiet time to consider who you can assist to feel joy in their own lives and then an area of understanding you would like to receive for yourself. Focus your resources in all forms to those who matter most to you and interact with them with your best self at all times.

With modern day distractions constantly within our lives if we choose to allow them in, seek to use your time with intention and purpose. Your body and mind will work best when we understand the natural cycles of energy and inspiration that cycle through us each day. Choose to start your day with joy and thanksgiving at another opportunity to create more joy in your life and in other people's lives. Work in the early part of your day towards your key feelings and actions that you wish to manifest in your life as quickly as possible, focusing on creating as similar conditions as possible to those goals.

Use the latter part of the day to refuel and recharge your mind and body, after the dedicated work portion of your day. Look after your mind and body as you would wish upon someone else, and understand fully how precious your internal mind and spirit is to allow you to take actions every day that fill you with happiness and joy. Aim to work no longer than is necessary, and give yourself more of what you feel is lacking in your life.

If you feel you are struggling with no time, give yourself more time to achieve one priority each day. If you feel you lack energy, do more than makes you come alive with fun and excitement and fuel your body correctly that it can turn the inside energy efficiently for movement and thoughts. If you lack respect from others, show respect to others first.

Whatever we believe we are lacking in the world, we must first give it out to the world in our actions for it then to be returned back to us, much like an eternal loop.

Principle 22: Develop a Master Morning Routine

Become excited for the life you are creating and arise early enough that you can be fully engaged in your most productive actions that make you feel joyful.

The Principle of a Master Morning Routine will change your life by setting your present day into alignment with an optimal version of yourself, aligned with your goals and desires. It is critical to wake up the mind and body in an optimal manner every day so that you can experience life to its fullest.

Seek to exercise your mind and body early for the day ahead, to maintain optimal physical and mental health, and include quiet, dedicated time to receive inspiration on what the day should involve. Our first priority should be to clean and prepare the body and mind for all what our heart's desires will be that day, using time as wisely as we can and including the best selection of fuel physically and mentally that we can currently find available to us. Giving our body that kick start to allow all the organs and brain to function from the first moments are critical, and nothing could be wiser than having a glass of room temperature water to hydrate your body right away. During the start of your day, your body will be looking to cleanse itself of any toxins and waste it was processing during your sleep, so be mindful to start your day with foods and sources of energy that will naturally make you feel good and allow your body to thrive.

Seek learning from the best books as early as you can in the day so that the inspirational words from others can be placed into your mind to ponder during the day's activities and drive new personal inspiration. A short time is only required to feel benefit from this simple action, and usually fifteen minutes is all that is needed in whatever form of hearing the stories from others that you prefer.

Finally, use the morning waking personal time to write in a personal journal that will act as a creation tool for what you want to manifest into your life through resources, and also allow you to clearly reflect and see evidence of this occurring to believe in its truthfulness more. Your morning writing should include initially one to three pages of writing from your mind without any pre-planned direction or intention. The action in this part of the Master Morning Routine and journaling is to allow you to free your subconscious mind from any distractions and to tune into what thoughts and promptings are there beneath the surface and have been developing whilst you slept.

Next, write down three aspects of your life you are currently grateful for and appreciate. If you are struggling with this, simply look after the room you are sitting in and describe the items that please you the most in three ways. Slowly, with daily effort, your response to this part of the Master Morning Routine will change from the items you see in front of you to the feelings you are experiencing in your life at that moment.

Plan for your day ahead wisely by next writing a list of actions, broken down into steps that are critical to achieve. This is very much like a classic "To Do" list for productivity. However, beside that short list you will write an additional column with the words "Universe To Do". Under the column on the right, in order to remove any worries or concerns from your mind and realise that you lack the power to control anything outside of your own personal mind, we write down any thoughts that are troubling you that you wish a solution to appear. With the act of writing it down, knowing that your life will open up a way to resolve it that requires no action from yourself, will give you immense joy. This right-hand column in this part of the Master Morning Routine will be one of the parts you look forward to the most each day as you hand over control for aspects of your life that you have no control over.

If you can, if any task would take only 3 minutes of your day to complete that is written on the personal to do list side of this action, do the action right there and then or take the first step towards action. The moment of inspiration is there for a reason to guide you on your path to the life you want, and it is our responsibility to act as quickly as possible on that guidance where it feels good to us to do so.

Next, we engage our imagination using Principle 15 in a creative way. Write down a gift of any large amount of money you feel would benefit your life if it were to appear that day out of the blue and detail exactly how you would spend it in whatever forms make you feel happy and bring joy to others. You will find that this action will draw money and resources to you to make these promptings happen far quicker than you could imagine.

Finally, write the word Inspiration in your journal entry for that day and leave plenty of blank space. Keep your journal with you often throughout the day so that as you feel inspiration arrive into your thoughts, and should you not be able to action right away, you have a location to write it down so that you can take action as soon as next available.

Principle 23: Develop an Eternal Evening Routine

This Principle will allow you to reflect and ponder on your daily actions to shape your future day ahead, and ideally works best when we commit to an evening routine every night. You can use this to connect with others as well for an even greater result in your life and their own.

Ponder and give thanks for what you have been given that day. Each day is a gift and our duty is to use it to seek out what brings us joy and fulfils our soul. Ideally write down your thoughts of gratitude in your personal journal so that you can track your life opening in ways you had not imagined where possible, and to allow any inspiration to be actioned right away the next day. This time should be treated as sacred to reflect, so keep distractions to a minimum and where possible, make it the very last thing you do before going to sleep so that the good joyful moments are visualised still in your mind and thoughts.

Share with a loved one your list of Micro-Joys experienced that day; the moments where you have been thankful and appreciate all you currently have and can see appearing in your life ahead. Encourage others to do the same so that they may feel the joy and happiness in their lives for a shared moment too.

Look to raise and encourage others with your new knowledge and experience learnt that day and what you have felt to be true.

Care for yourself so you can face the day tomorrow stronger and wiser. The time before sleep should be used to relax your mind naturally so that your sleep can be productive and restore your energy and spirit for the following day with excitement. Consider eliminating anything that acts as a distraction to take you from achieving the best sleep that you can. If you feel you have stresses or worries on your mind, use this time to write down those thoughts in your journal but then also write down beside them the worst-case scenario and then how you would counteract that situation with new habits. Turn any negative thoughts into a positive plan of action and you will release the control fear and uncertainty has over you.

Give proper care for your shelter and home items in a way that you would wish it to be treated, as they are another relationship that we must maintain, and prepare as much as you can for the day you have planned tomorrow so that your attention can be on your thoughts positively rather than distracted.

Review what you could have done better and write down one alternative way you could have handled the situation if you had been aware of the long-term outcomes instead of the short-term feelings.

Right any wrongs before going to bed so that you can sleep deep and sound, knowing that you are at peace and have closure from the day left behind.

Principle 24: Seek learning always from those who are happy and successful.

The greatest gift to your present-day self and future self is actively choosing how we wish to feel and taking action daily that allow us to have those feelings. This action alone will allow us to become far greater that we imagined possible.

There is nothing new under the sun with many successful principles already communicated to us, and in order that we can grow and develop, it is our primary objective to first feel and respond to our thoughts that fill us with joy, but also to seek out the ways as much as possible that can make that happen.

Learn from the best books of the wisest and happiest people who have lived and are currently living. Only through experience can we truly learn what we hold to as our core principles, and by learning and studying the words of others who have had that experience will allow us to bypass any of the mental or physical struggle taken to reach that enlightenment.

Learn and grow each day to become the greatest version of ourselves that we can.

PART 3:

OUR FUTURE

Our Freedom Fuelled FUTURE

Your future will be determined by your present actions, thoughts and feelings without fail. Therefore, it must be a considered choice each day about the life you want to lead and how you wish to feel.

Whilst we live each day seeking after our joy as our priority, listening to our intuition as a guide and taking action consistently, there are a few principles we can add as finer details to our present day, specifically to shape our future with faith and certainty as to the abundance we deserve and know will remain present.

Principle 25: The Law of the Vital Few

The age-less principle of the Law of the Vital Few remains as true today as it was in the past, whereby applying a few key principles, we will receive the majority of the possible success and abundance due to us. With regards to money and our future, aiming for a minimum of twenty percent of your current income being used for future income creating purposes, knowing you have exchanged yourself working for money for the money working for you in the future, will allow you to use this law and see the positive results accordingly.

Trusting and believing that some of our current wealth should be intended to actively work for us and be invested for our future will allow us to create passive incomes that are generated automatically in our sleep indefinitely. Give a portion of wealth to successful others who have proved their business growth consistently in the past and find opportunities to invest allow your wealth to grow as much as possible for your return. Allow them to become wealthy and grow their business, but use the eighth wonder of the world that is compound interest to create an opportunity for you to have a solid income source too. The power of compound interest will allow your wealth to grow exponentially whilst you sleep to enjoy during your future days.

Only you will truly have your best financial and time intentions as the priority, and so with any investment you make, with any resource you control, ensure that you take full responsibility for where you store or place that resource for safe keeping to use at a later time.

Set aside also a portion of your current wealth to pursue any inspirational ideas regarding business that that you feel good about and can see a vision of helping others greatly. Seek out ways to help others get everything they want in life, and they will ensure you have everything you want through the value you have brought them.

Principle 26: Give to yourself and others fully

Your own personal development is the greatest gift you can give your children and loved ones, along with your time and love. Give these fully and give due attention to them so they can connect with you and build everlasting relationships built upon the true principles of care and commitment. Self-sacrifice and putting your needs last for others will teach no useful lessons to anyone and only lead to negative emotions and experiences for you and your loved ones. Children copy and learn from what they see, and it should be our highest priority to show others in our family or life in general the standard we hold for ourselves and we believe anyone can achieve.

Giving to others allows us to be fully human and become bigger than just our external possessions. The more we pour out to others with all our resources including money, the more we allow life to pour in more joy and happiness back to us. Giving away some of our resources will also allow us to achieve financial and time freedom sooner, as more opportunities will be provided to you to return the money and multiplied. Always give to others with the intention to help others who are suffering, and do this not for the promised return, but to help, others knowing we have been given much already in our lives to be thankful for.

Money allows us to make a real difference to those around us and strangers alike, as it can lift them from their current experience to reconnect with the higher mindset that we know is available to them if they choose to see it once more.

The primary focus in our lives should be to seek after long lasting joy by being fully present with our thoughts and actions. Live life with passion and gratitude, and your deepest dreams will be fulfilled with all the resources the world has to offer.

CLOSING THOUGHTS

And with the end of this book, your own journey using the Master Money Blueprint has only just begun.

You may have experienced many moments of enlightenment as you read through all the principles and committed to action.

Lasting change does not occur from reading alone, but use the principles in this book as an invitation to continue to seek out the thoughts and feelings that bring joy and happiness to you every day. Money is one energy source that we can use to shape our lives into what we want them to be, and life has blessed us with many more sources to master and use wisely for that sole purpose.

Seek to practice daily the principles that feel good to you and help others feel the same joy in their lives in whatever way you can.

This is the start of your greatest adventure ahead.

ABOUT THE AUTHOR

Scottish Award-winning Money and Success Blogger/Youtube Creator Jennifer Kempson is recognised as one of the leading and most insightful voices within the UK Financial Freedom and Debt-free community under the brand name of "Mamafurfur".

A Member of the Institute of Engineering and Technology and a STEM (Science Technology Engineering Mathematics) Ambassador, she balances her life shared with her family with her passion to help others achieve financial and time freedom through sharing smarter money and lifestyle habits principles. Her passion is to help others use money as their tool to create the life they truly want with flexibility and joy.

Winner of the UK Money Bloggers Community (https://ukmoneybloggers.com/) "Best Money Vlogger (Youtube Creator Channel) 2018" voted by her UK Money creator peers, with a technical background of a Master of Engineering in Electronics and Electrical Engineering (European) from University of Glasgow, you can find Jennifer online at www.mamafurfur.com or on Youtube by searching for Mamafurfur.

For all enquiries or questions, she can be contacted via the common social media platforms under the name of @Mamafurfur.

Printed in Great Britain
by Amazon

47022045R00047